Juniper and Rose
Coloring and Activity Book Two

Illustrated by Alexandra Gold
Designed by FindlayCreative.com

Dara Publishing
Read, Enlighten, Empower, Aspire.

www.darapublishing.co

Visit our website and follow us on social media.

Dedicated to:
This coloring and activity book is dedicated to Dedication.

Number Finder

Junpier and Rose are working on a number finder. Use the numbers down the side of the page to replace the missing numbers in the puzzle. Cross out the numbers when you find a place for them.

1	2	3	4	5

3	4	5		7

6		8	9	

4		6	7	8

2		4	5	6

5	6	7		

3
9
~~1~~
7
6
5
8
10

4

The Star Maze

When you wish upon a star... Help Juniper and Rose reach the star.
Don't forget to make a wish!

Start Here

Word Puzzle

Juniper and Rose are preparing to cook and they need your help to find what they need to prepare a delicious meal. Find the words listed beside the puzzle, and circle the words you find. Now... let's get cooking!

r	o	s	e	b	c	j
x	c	p	o	t	u	u
q	o	o	s	z	p	n
f	o	o	j	u	g	i
o	k	n	i	f	e	p
o	p	l	a	t	e	e
d	b	o	w	l	z	r

Find these cooking words!

cook
juniper
spoon
bowl
knife
cup
pot
plate
rose
food
jug

Fill in the Blanks

Juniper and Rose are playing but it is time for dinner. Complete each sentence using the words in the suggestion box to find out what the story says.

They shrieked "No!" in the __morning__ during _____. Their "No!" echoed _____ down the hallway, and traveled _____ the staircase.

morning / loudly / down / breakfast

8

Connect the Dots

Juniper and Rose are making dinner tonight! Connect the dots to
find out what they are cooking for dinner. Start at number 1
and join each dot to reveal the picture.

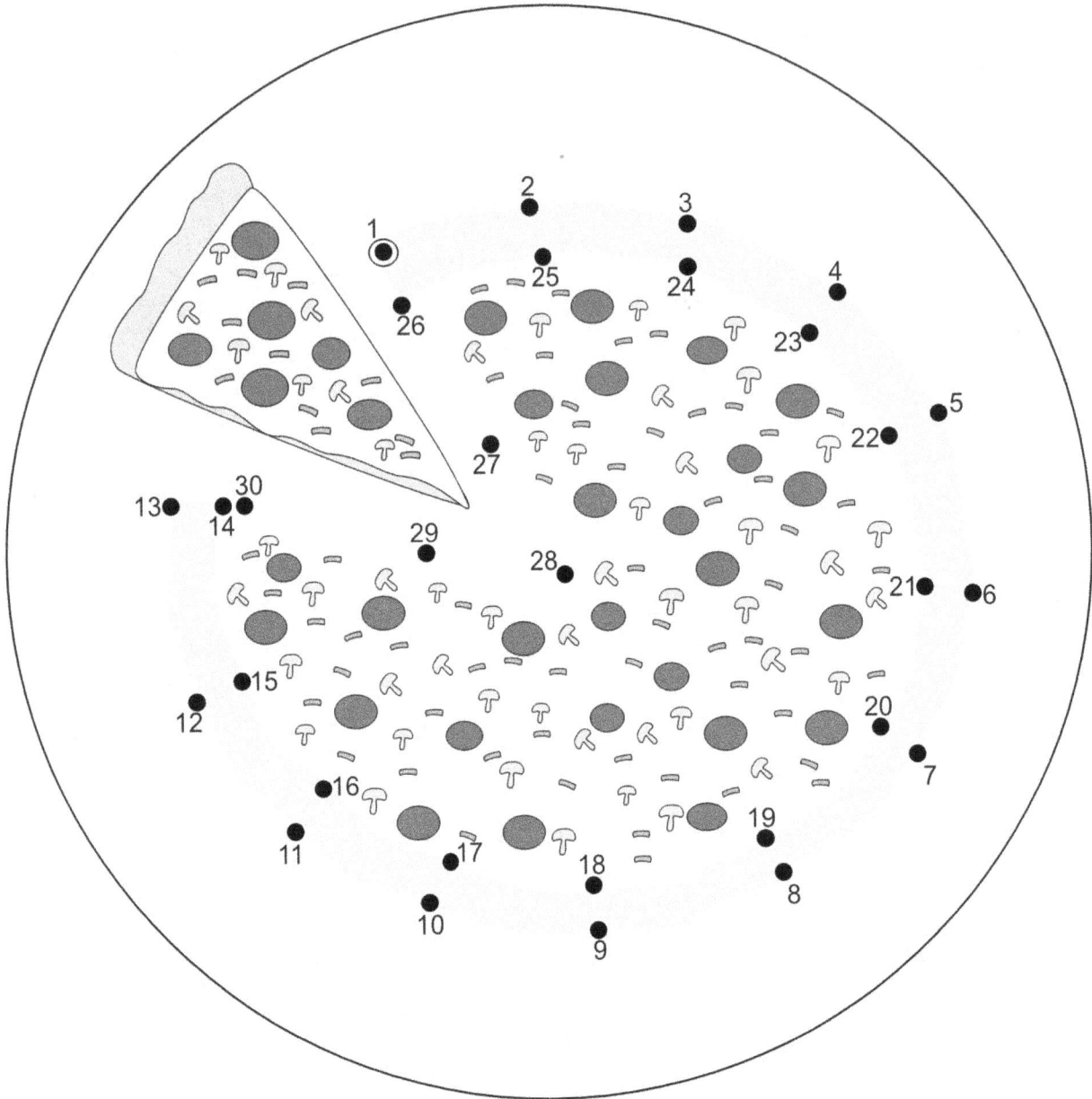

Cup Cake Maze

Morning tea time! Help Juniper and Rose by following the maze
until you find their missing cup cake.

Start Here

Color by Numbers

Time for some more numbers! Use the key below to color the different types of fruit in the fruit bowl. When you are finished, your picture will be complete. Enjoy!

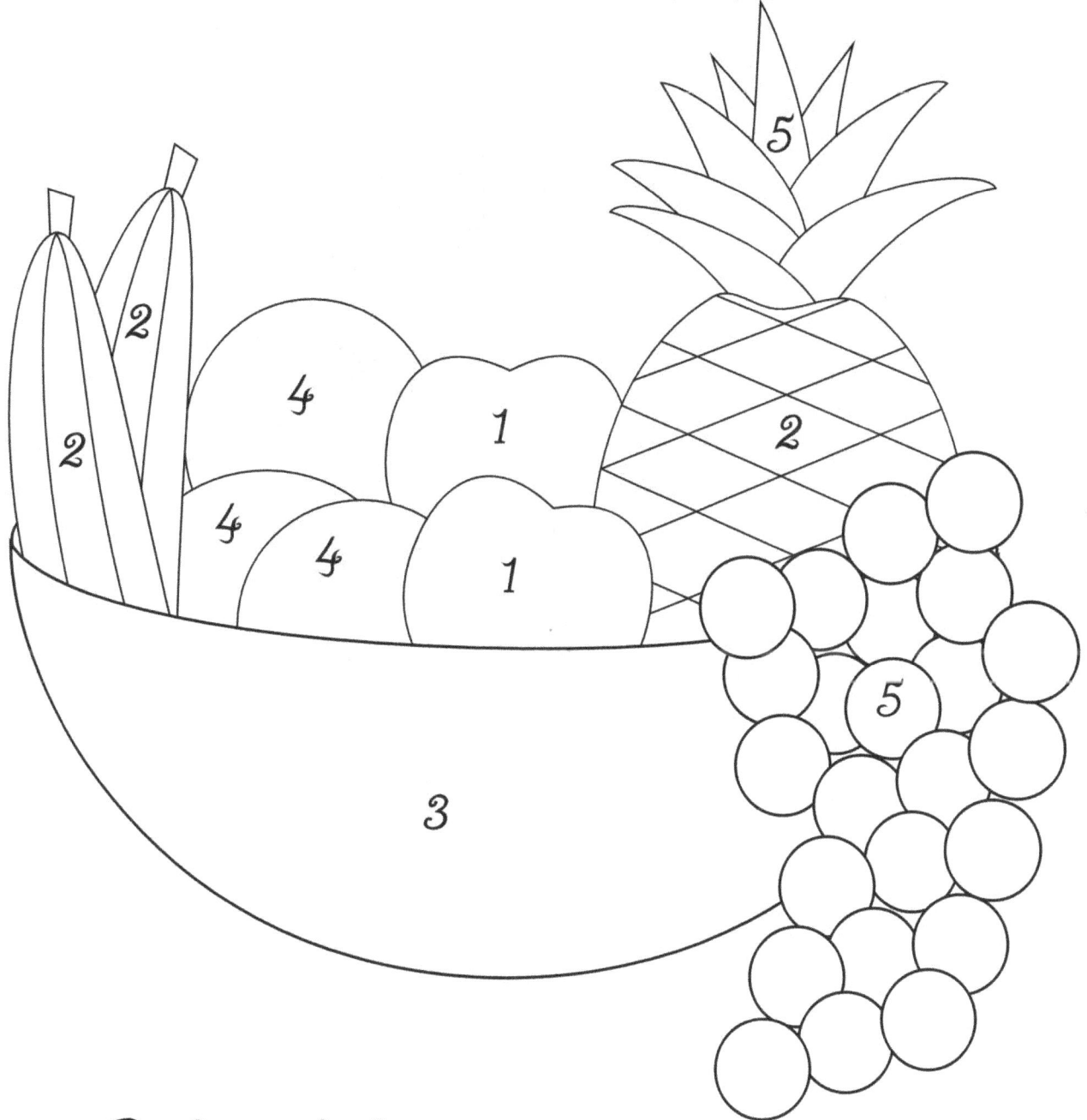

Color Key:
1. Red   2. Yellow   3. Blue
4. Orange   5. Green

Spot the Difference

There are ten differences; can you spot them in these pictures?

Fill in the Blanks

It is dessert time. Complete the sentence using the words in the suggestion box to find out what the story says.

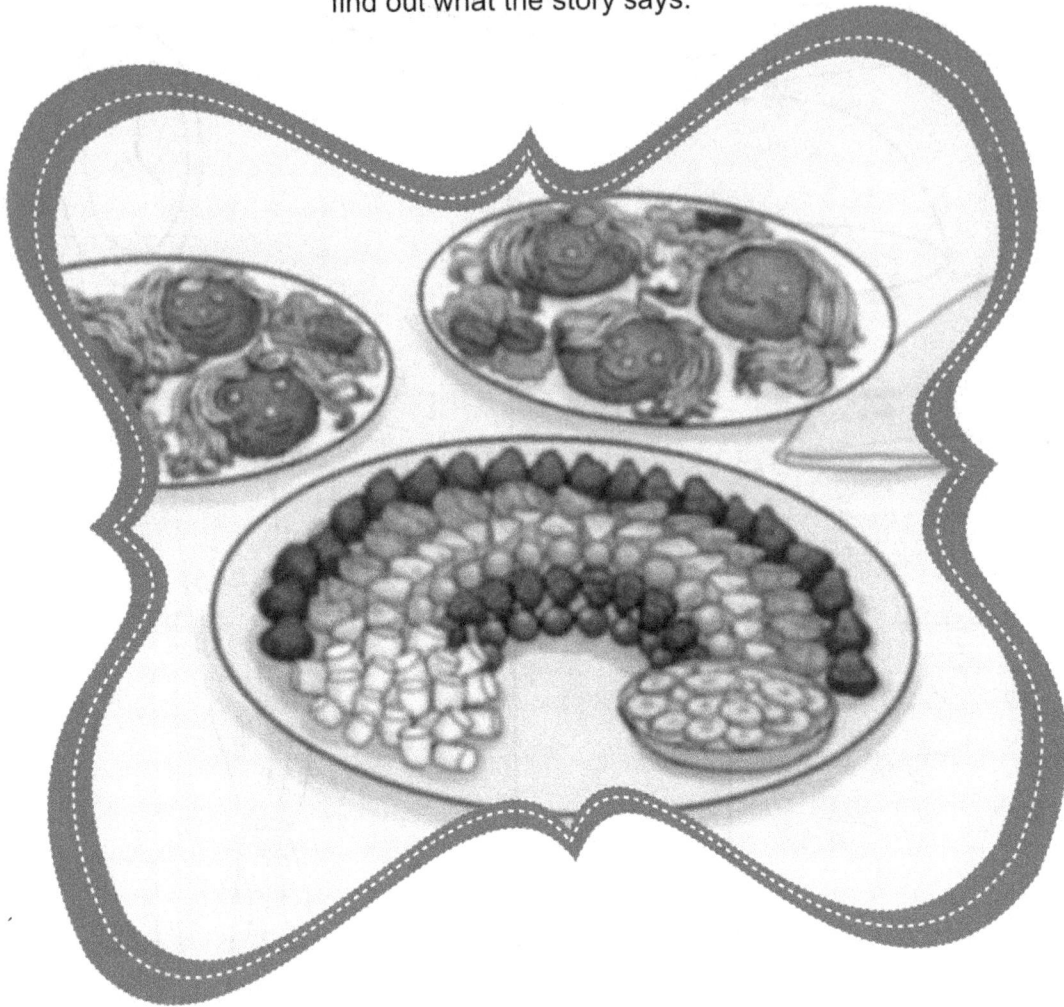

_____ **Mom** chuckled. "Yes. _____, we're having a _____ rainbow with marshmallow and _____ clouds."

Mom / banana / fruit / Tonight

16

Fruit Rainbow Maze

Juniper and Rose are collecting ingredients to make their favorite Rainbow Fruit Salad. Can you help them get the last of their ingredients? Follow the maze until you reach the pineapple.

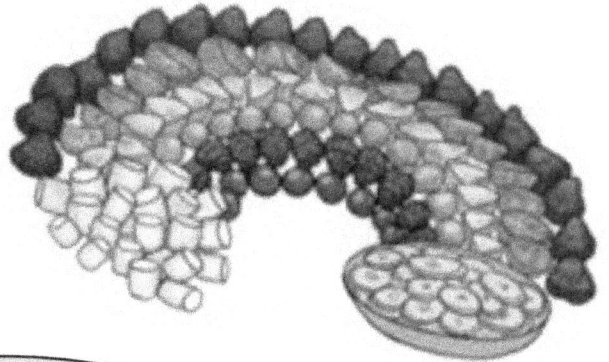

Start Here

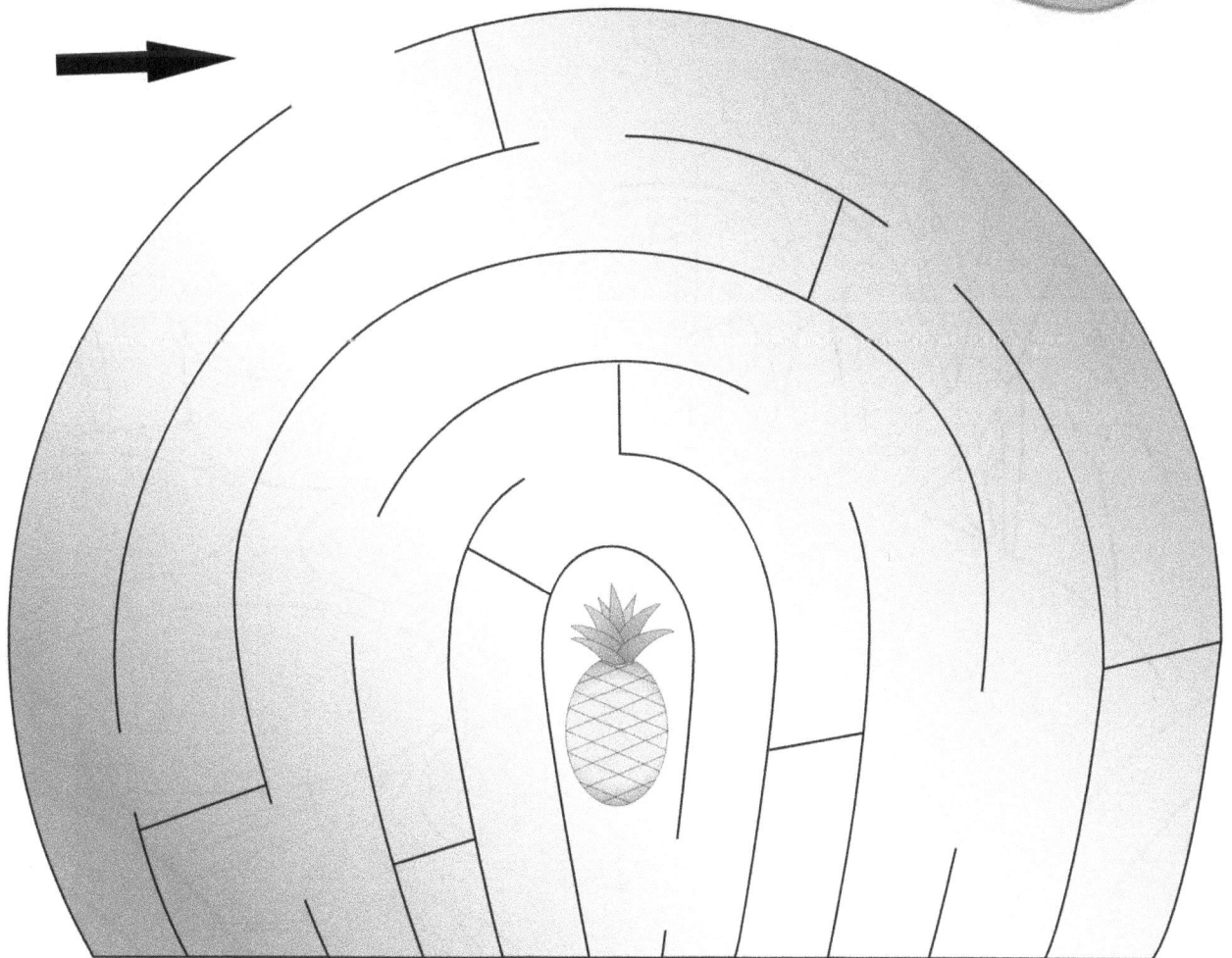

Word Finder

Have a go by crossing out each of the letters that appear more than once. Write the remaining letters down to solve the puzzle.

c d   w t

o ~~i~~ n b l p v l

b t d p a j z v

h r j u ~~i~~ k e q

u j z c q ~~i~~ l k

g k   w h

Write the answer below!

_ _ _ _ _ _ _ _

19

Number Finder

Use the numbers down the side of the page to replace the missing
numbers in the puzzle. Cross out each number when
you find a place for them.

5	4	3		1

7	6		4	3

6	5	4		2

10	9		7	6

	8	7	6	5

8			6	5	

9
3
~~6~~
8
4
5
2
7

Spot the Difference

There are ten differences; can you spot them in these pictures?

Connect the Dots

Tea party time! Connect the dots to find Juniper and
Rose's tea cups. Start at number 1 and
join each dot to reveal the picture.

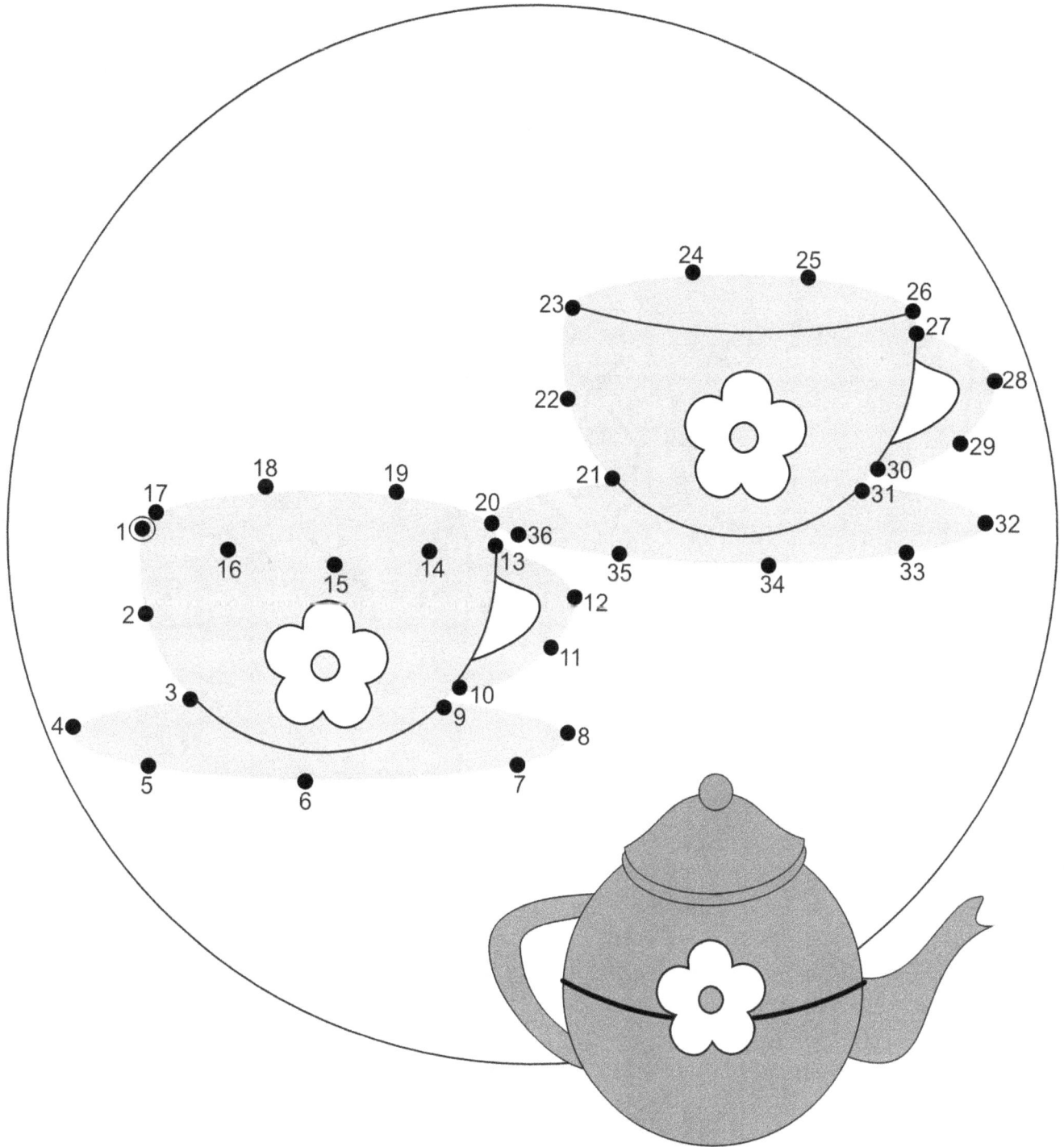

24 25

23 26
27

22 28

29

18 19 21 30
17 20 31
1 36
16 14 13 35 32
15 12
2 34 33

11

3 10

4 9 8

5 6 7

Fill in the Blanks

Juniper and Rose are ready for dinner. Complete the sentence using the words in the suggestion box to find out what Juniper and Rose are struggling with.

So, after a **long** _____ day filled with lots of _____

and _____ Juniper and _____

realized that it was almost dinnertime.

```
long  /  laughter  /  fun  /  Rose
```

Which Shape is This?

It is shape time! Can you help Juniper and Rose find out
what the name of each shape is? Draw a line
from each shape to its correct name.

1

2

3

4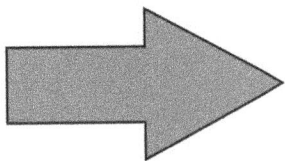

5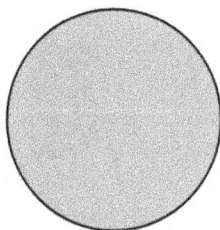

A Circle

B Triangle

C Heart

D Star

E Arrow

Word Puzzle

There are a lot of delivious fruits in this puzzle. Can you find them?
Search for the fruits listed beside the puzzle,
and circle the words you find.

```
o r a n g e a
k d p e a r p
i a p l u m r
w t l i m e i
i e e f i g c
b a n a n a o
b e r r y n t
```

Find these fruit!

apple
orange
banana
kiwi
apricot
berry
plum
date
lime
fig
pear

The Golden Fish Maze

Juniper and Rose are making Golden Fish for lunch. Follow around the maze to find the last orange slice for their yummy recipe.

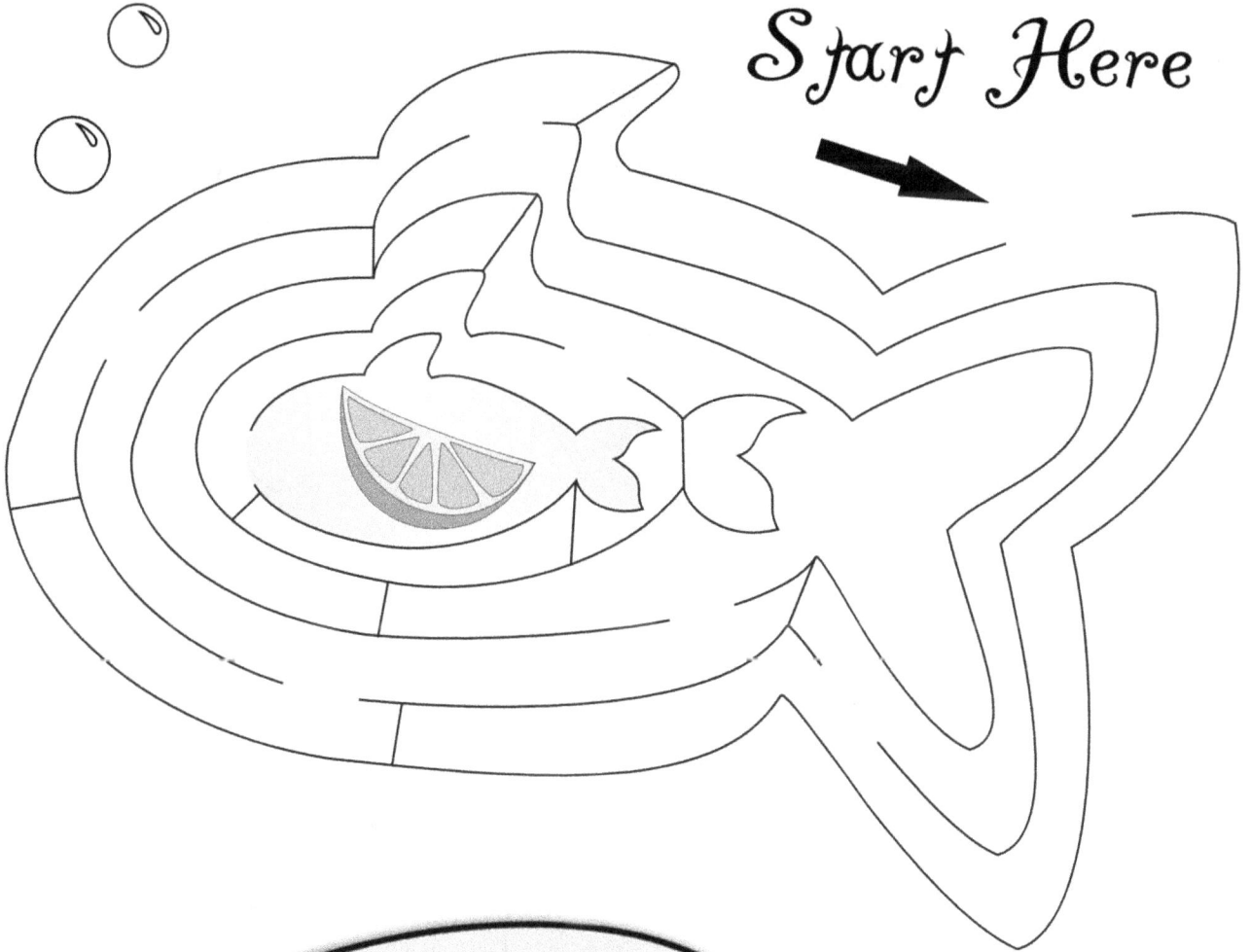

Start Here

Connect the Dots

Connect the dots from 1 to 33 to discover which fruit are in the
fruit bowl. Start at number 1 and join each dot
to reveal the picture.

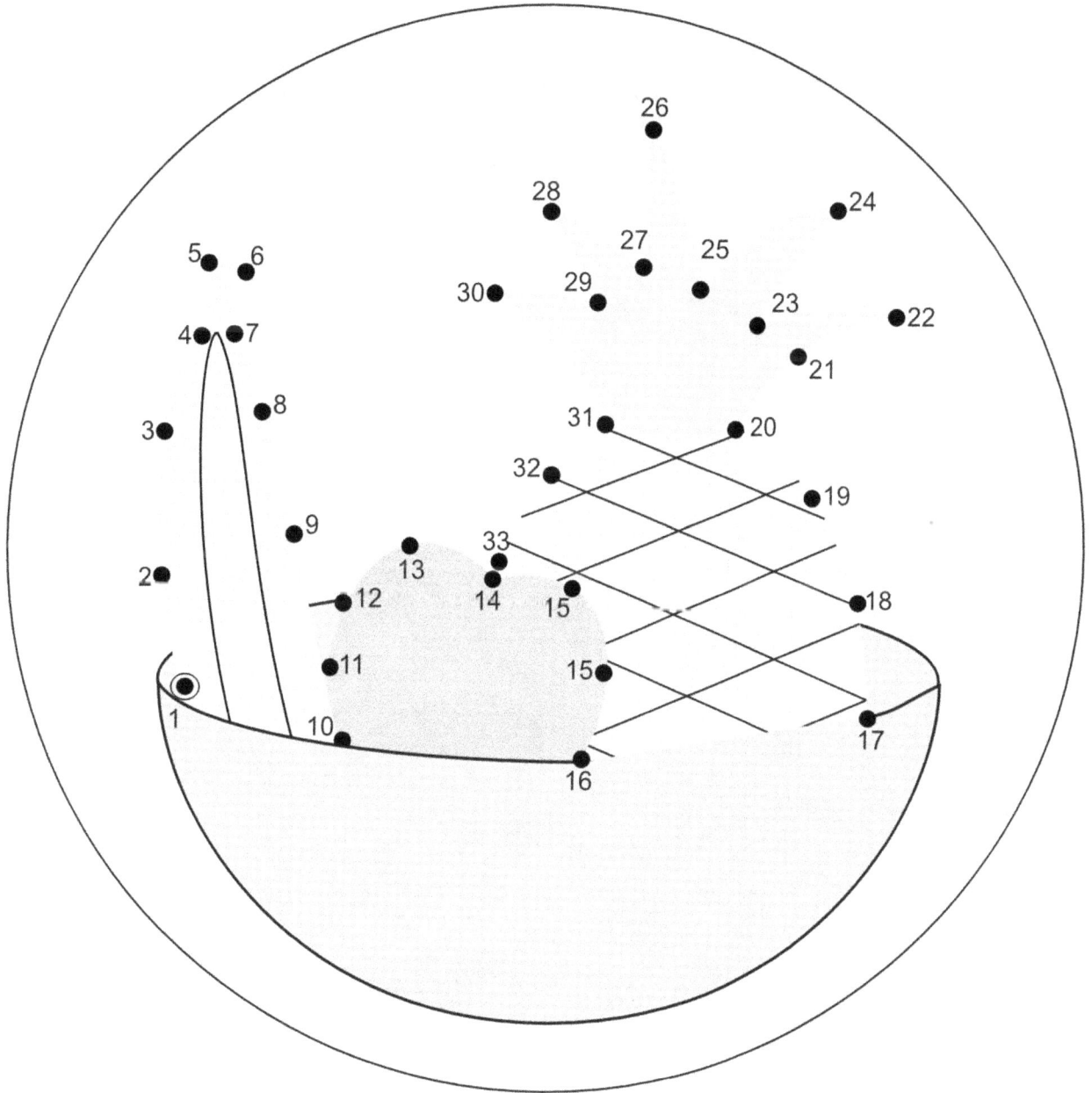

26
28
24
5 6
27 25
30 29 23
4 7 22
21
8
3
31 20
32 19
9
33
13
2
12 14 15 18
11 15
10 17
1 16

31

Spot the Difference

There are ten differences; can you spot them in these pictures?

Color by Numbers

Baking time! Juniper and Rose have collected all the equipment they
will need to bake a cake. Use the key below to color the picture.
Once you are finished, your picture will be complete.

Color Key:
1. Yellow 2. Green 3. Purple
4. Pink 5. Blue

Word Finder

What are the girls up to today? Let's find out by crossing out each of the letters that appear more than once. Write the remaining letters down to solve the puzzle.

```
j  r              w  d
o  e  n  w  l  x  s  q
b  t  d  y  x  t  j  v
y  m̶  s  c  i  a  e  q
r  c  g  c  m̶  s  l  k
x  o              w  s
```

Write the answer below!

_ _ _ _ _ _ _ _

35

Fill in the Blanks

Dinner times were such a struggle for Mom and Dad.
Complete each sentence using the words in the
suggestion box to find out what the story says.

During mealtime, Mom and __**Dad**__ had to
constantly _____ them: "One _____
bite, _____..."

Dad / **more** / **please** / **encourage**

Connect the Dots

Connect the dots to find out which fruit Juniper and Rose need for their Lion Pancake recipe. Start at number 1 and join each dot to reveal the picture.

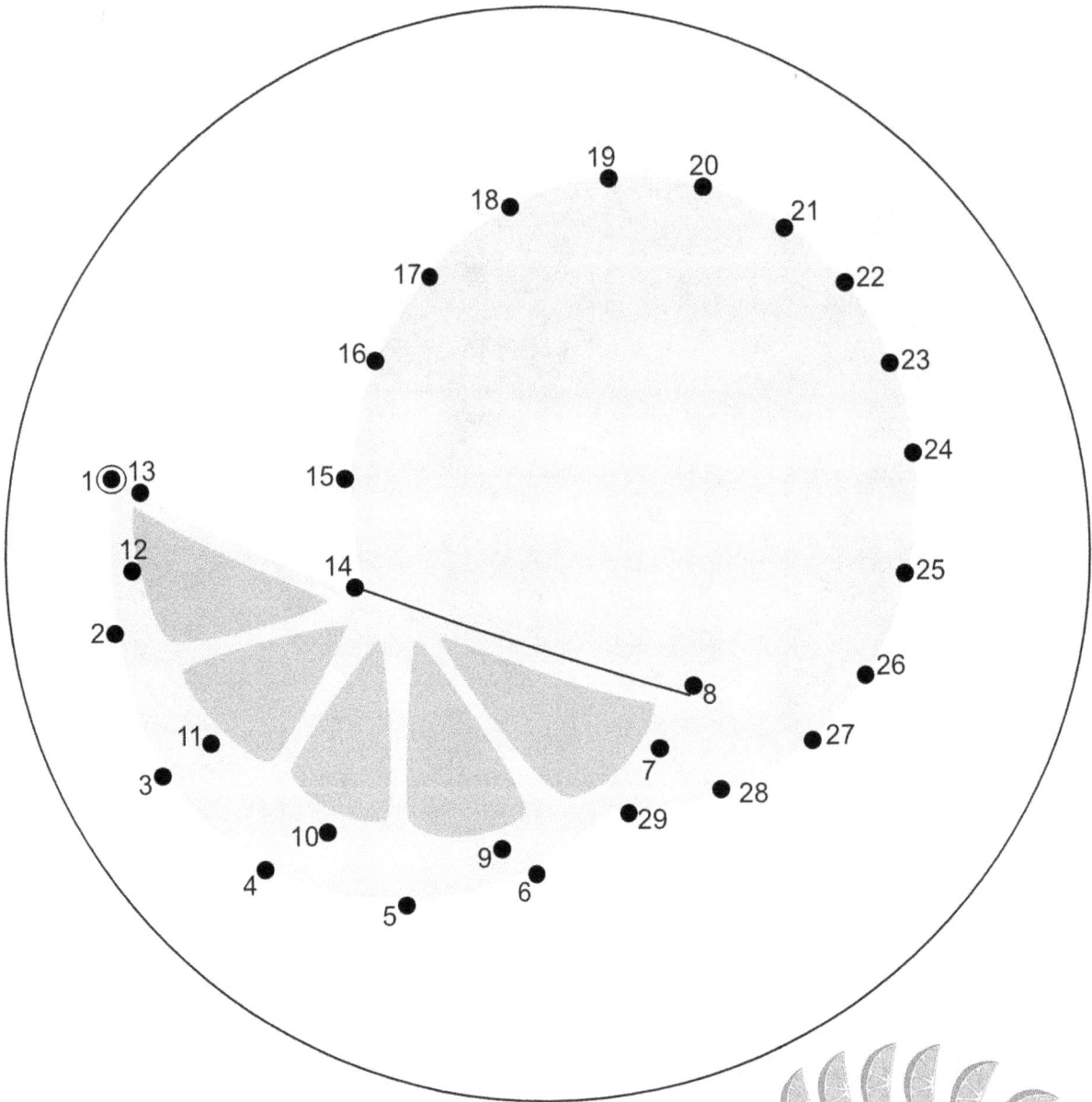

Word Puzzle

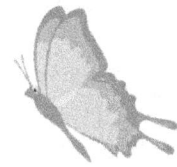

This puzzle is all about vetegables.
Search for the vegetables listed beside the puzzle,
and circle the words you find. Find these vegetables!

```
c a r r o t l
e y a m b o e
l k d p e m t
e a i e a a t
r l s a n t u
y e h s s o c
p e p p e r e
```

Find these colors!

pepper
carrot
celery
rashish
lettuce
yam
tomato
beans
peas
kale

Spot the Difference

There are ten differences; can you spot them in these pictures?

Fill in the Blanks

The twins refused to eat. Complete each sentence using the words in the suggestion box to find out what the story says.

No matter how ___hard___ Mom and Dad tried,

_____ and Rose wouldn't

take _____ more _____.

hard / bite / one / Juniper

Color by Numbers

Juniper and Rose have been baking! Can you color the picture
below by using the number key provided?
Let's get coloring!

Color Key:
1. Blue 2. Green 3. Pink
4. Yellow 5. Red

The Apple Maze

It's snack time and Juniper and Rose want an apple. Can you
help them get it? Follow the maze until you reach
the apple. The girls will surely be grateful.

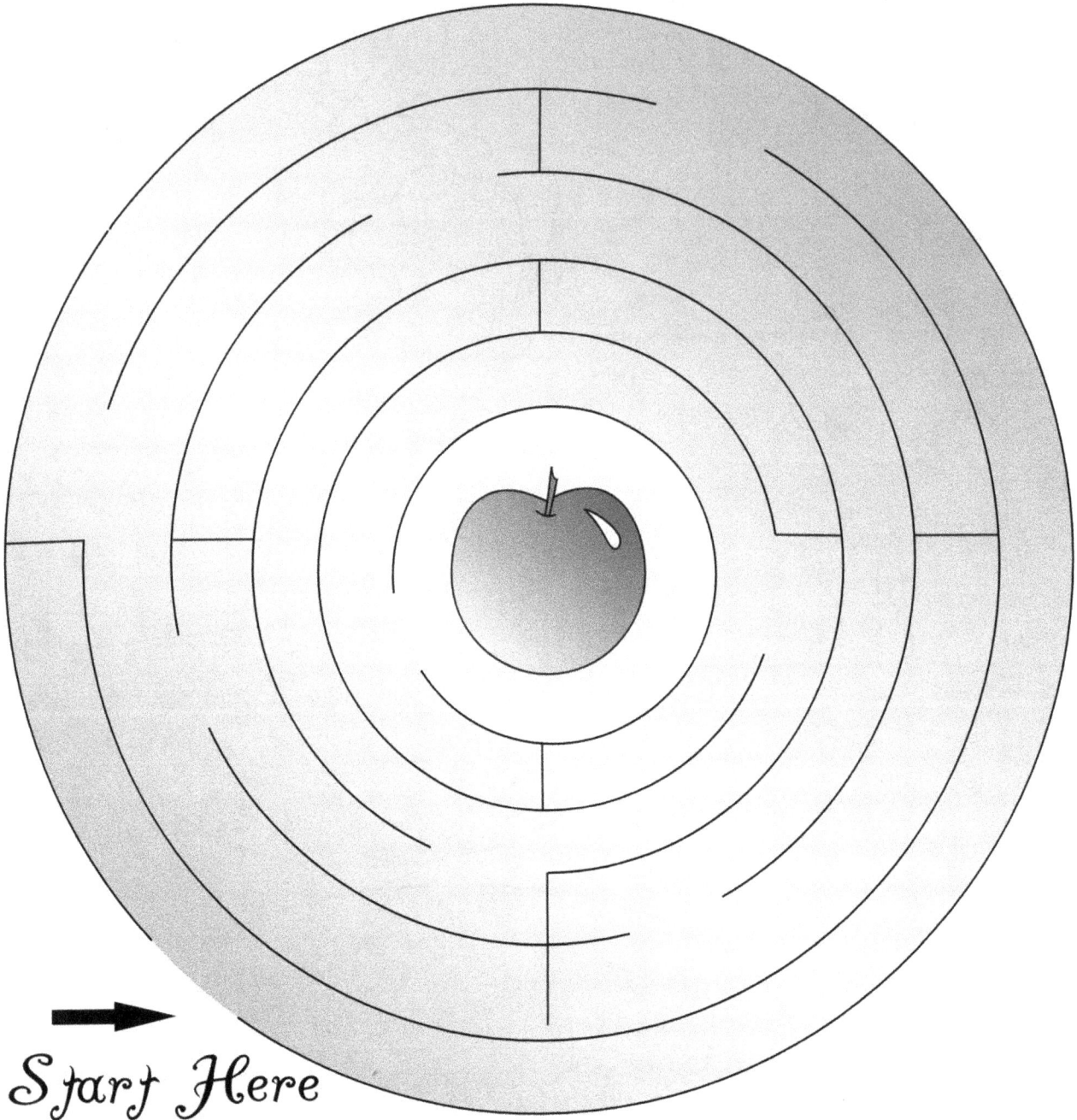

Start Here

Match the Number

Count the number of shapes in each box then draw a line
from each box to its correct number.

1

2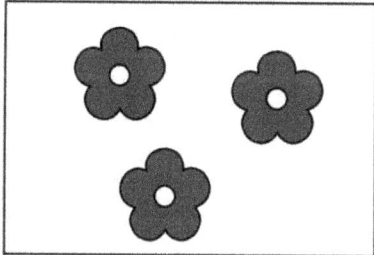

3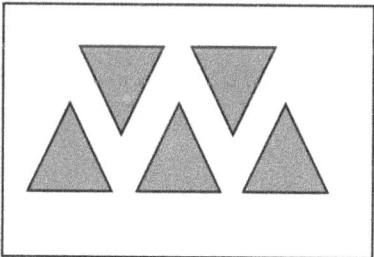

4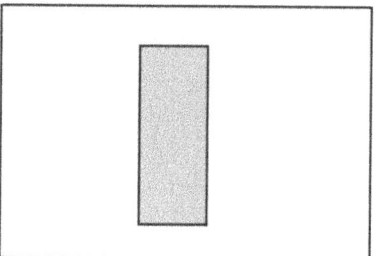

5

A Five

B Three

C One

D Four

E Two

Fill in the Blanks

It is play time! Complete the sentence using the words in the suggestion box to find out what the story says.

"No, **Mommy** _____! We're still _____."

Juniper and Rose didn't _____

much about _____.

Mommy / eating / care / playing

Word Finder

Juniper and Rose are working on a word finder. Have a go yourself by crossing out each of the letters that appear more than once. Write the remaining letters down to solve the puzzle.

o p   k n

g ~~b~~ f w e m t l

w i p m a j h r

h a n u ~~b~~ d e q

k j c o q a l d

g o   k c

Write the answer below!

_ _ _ _ _

Connect the Dots

Connect the dots to find out what Juniper and Rose are baking today for morning tea! Start at number 1 and join each dot to reveal the picture. Enjoy!

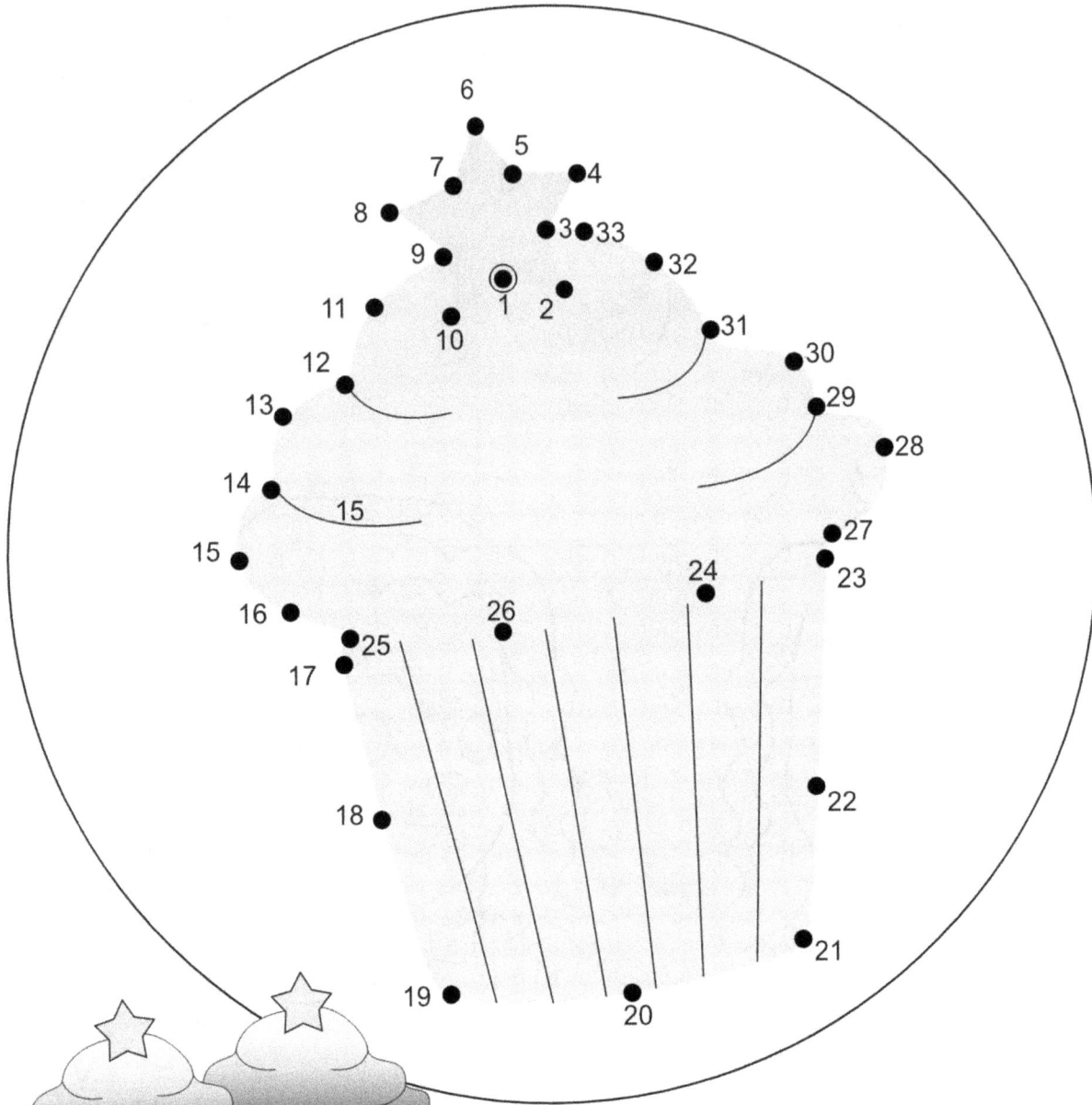

The Lion Maze

Juniper and Rose have been cooking again.
Follow the maze until you reach the Lion pancake.

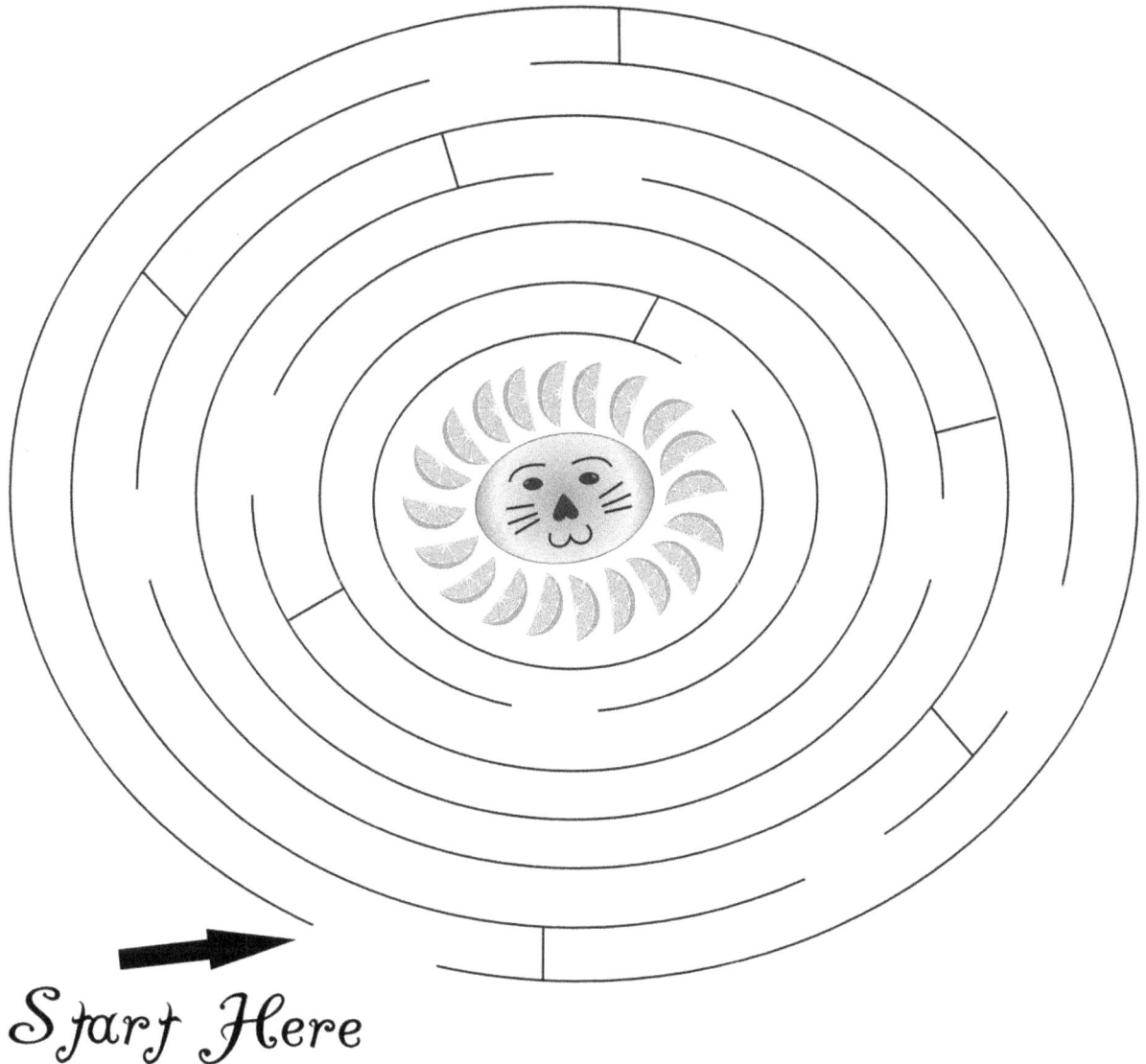

Start Here

Juniper and Rose
Answer Page

Page 4
Number Finder Solution:

1	2	3	4	5
3	4	5	6	7
6	7	8	9	10
4	5	6	7	8
2	3	4	5	6
5	6	7	8	9

Page 5
Maze Solution:

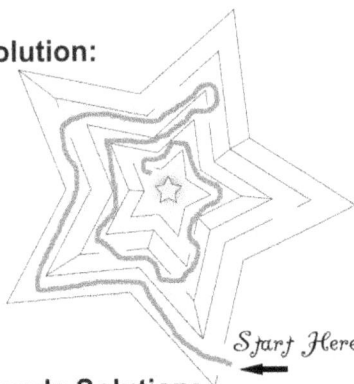

Start Here

Page 7
Word Puzzle Solution:

Page 8
Fill in the Blanks Solution:

They shrieked "No!" in the
__morning__ during __breakfast__.
Their "No!" echoed __loudly__
down the hallway, and traveled
__down__ the staircase.

Page 10
Connect the Dots Solution:

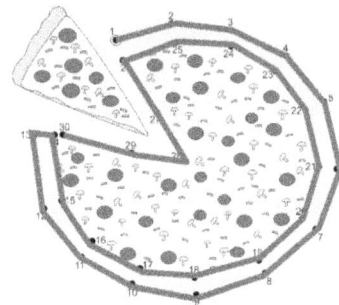

Page 11
Cup Cake Maze Solution

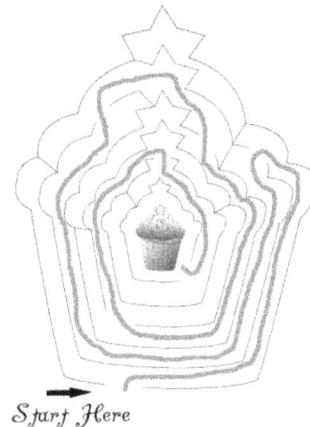

Start Here

Page 14
Spot the Difference Solution:

54

Juniper and Rose

Answer Page Continued

Page 16
Fill in the Blanks Solution:

_____Mom_____ chuckled. "Yes, _____tonight_____,
we're having a _____fruit_____ rainbow
with marshmellow and _____banana_____
clouds."

Page 17
Fruit Rainbow Maze Solution:

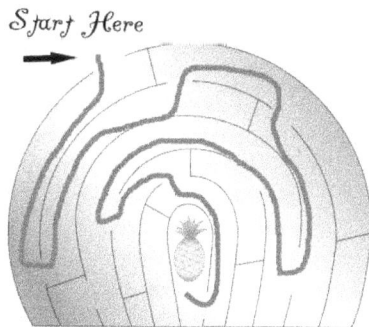

Page 19
Word Finder Answer: orange

Page 20
Number Finder Solution

5	4	3	**4**	1
7	6	**5**	4	3
6	5	4	**3**	2
10	9	**8**	7	**6**
9	8	7	6	5
8	**7**	6	5	**4**

Page 22
Spot the Difference Solution:

Page 23
Connect the Dots Solution:

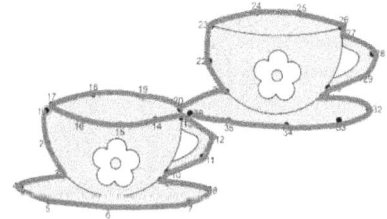

Page 25
Fill in the Blanks Solution:

So, after a _____long_____ day filled with lots of
_____fun_____ and _____laughter_____, Juniper and
_____Rose_____ realised that it was
almost dinnertime."

Page 26
What Shape is This Solution:

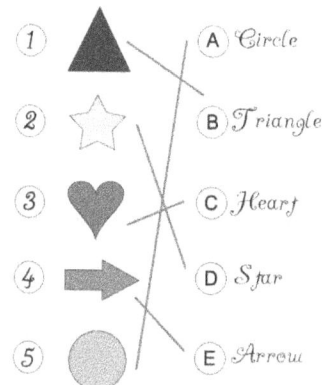

Juniper and Rose
Answer Page Continued

Page 28
Word Puzzle Solution:

Page 29
Golden Fish Maze Solution:

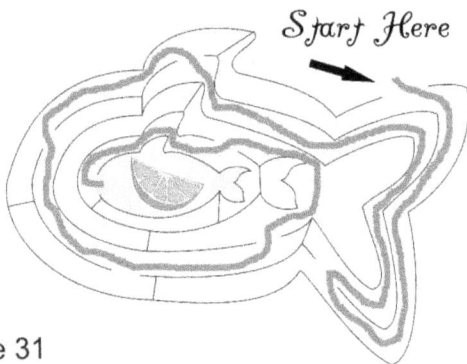

Start Here

Page 31
Connect the Dots Solution:

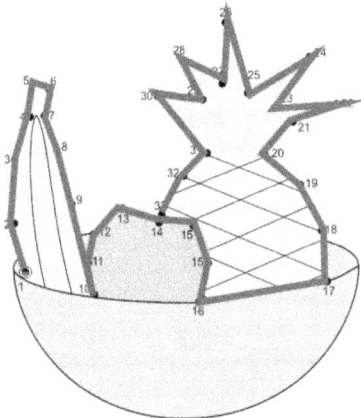

Page 32
Spot the Difference Solution:

Page 35
Word Finder Answer: baking

Page 37
Fill in the Blanks Solution:

During mealtime, mom and __Dad__ had to constantly ___encourage___ them. "One ___more___ bite, ___please___."

Page 38
Connect the Dots Solution:

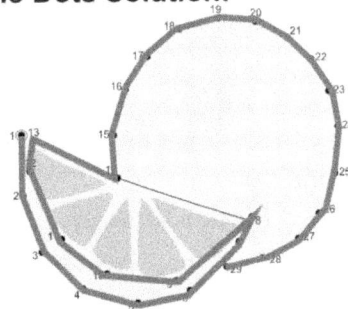

Page 40
Word Puzzle Solution:

56

Juniper and Rose
Answer Page Continued

Page 41
Spot the Difference Solution:

Page 43
Fill in the Blanks Solution:

No matter how ___hard___ Mom and Dad tried, ___Juniper___ and Rose wouldn't take ___one___ more ___bite___.

Page 46
Apple Maze Solution:

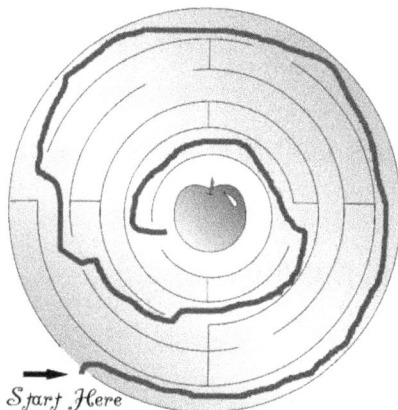

Start Here

Page 47
Match the Numbers Solution:

1 — E Two
2 — D Four
3 — B Three
4 — C One
5 — A Five

Page 49
Fill in the Blanks Solution:

"No, ___Mommy___! We're still ___playing___.' Juniper and Rose didn't ___care___ much about ___eating___.

Page 50
Word Finder Answer: fruit

Page 52
Connect the Dots Solution:

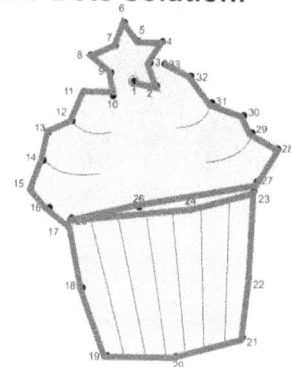

Page 53
Lion Maze Solution:

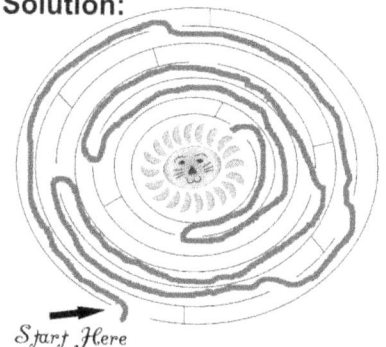

Start Here

ABOUT THE AUTHOR

In addition to being a mom, Reea is also a full time Childcare Provider, or "Nanny," and has dedicated herself to bringing joy, safety, trust and, most importantly, love to her extended families. Her passion for her work and her desire to help children inspired Reea to write children's books that will be useful in building character. She wants to assist not only the children she cares for with daily issues they may be facing, but kids all over the world. Being both a mom and a nanny allows her to view various situations through a child's perspective, throughout different stages of life. Subjects including fear, separation anxiety, behavioral problems, bravery, imagination, witty personality, love, compassion and teamwork are all wonderful inspirations for her children's story and activity books.

"I know in my heart that my future lies in sharing my stories with children in every walk of life, all over the world." –Reea Rodney

Want to connect with Dara Publishing / Reea Rodney?
Visit: www.darapublishing.co

For more FREE Juniper and Rose activities visit her activities page.

And Reea is also on social media at
www.facebook.com/darapublishing